WHO?

Matumayini Lilia
Mboleza

BALBOA.PRESS
A DIVISION OF HAY HOUSE

Balboa Press books may be ordered through booksellers or by contacting:

Balboa Press
A Division of Hay House
1663 Liberty Drive
Bloomington, IN 47403
www.balboapress.com.au
AU TFN: 1 800 844 925 (Toll Free inside Australia)
AU Local: 0283 107 086 (+61 2 8310 7086 from outside Australia)

Print information available on the last page.

ISBN: 978-1-5043-2091-7 (sc)
ISBN: 978-1-5043-2092-4 (e)

Balboa Press rev. date: 02/24/2020

Introduction

Who= who's who is; who has.

pronoun; possessive whose; objective whom.

what person or persons?: Who did it?

(of a person) of what character, origin, position, importance, etc.: Who does she think she is?

the person that or any person that (used relatively to represent a specified or implied antecedent): It was who you thought.

(used relatively in restrictive and non-restrictive clauses to represent a specified antecedent, the antecedent being a person or sometimes an animal or personified thing): Any kid who wants to can learn to swim.

Archaic. the person or persons who.

Questions For Anyone May Ask Yourself Or Someone Else

IT IS AN ABUNDANCE TO ASK QUESTION.

IT IS AN ACCOUNTABILITY TO ASK QUESTION.

IT IS AN ACCOMPLISHMENT TO ASK QUESTION.

IT IS AN ACCOMPLISH TO ASK QUESTION.

IT IS AN ACCURACY TO ASK QUESTION.

IT IS AN ACHIEVEMENT TO ASK QUESTION.

IT IS AN ACHIEVE TO ASK QUESTION.

IT IS AN ACKNOWLEDGEMENT TO ASK QUESTION.

IT IS AN ADAPTABILITY TO ASK QUESTION.

IT IS AN ADVENTURE TO ASK QUESTION.

IT IS AN ADVENTUROUS TO ASK QUESTION.

IT IS AN AGILITY TO ASK QUESTION.

IT IS AN ALERTNESS TO ASK QUESTION.

IT IS AN AMBITION TO ASK QUESTION.

IT IS AN ANTICIPATION TO ASK QUESTION.

IT IS AN APPRECIATE TO ASK QUESTION.

IT IS AN APPRECIATION TO ASK QUESTION.

IT IS AN APPRECIATIVE TO ASK QUESTION.

IT IS AN APPRECIATIVENESS TO ASK QUESTION.

IT IS AN ASSERTIVENESS TO ASK QUESTION.

IT IS AN ASSERTIVE TO ASK QUESTION.

IT IS AN ATTENTIVENESS TO ASK QUESTION.

IT IS AN AUDACITY TO ASK QUESTION.

IT IS AN AWARE TO ASK QUESTION.

IT IS AN AWARENESS TO ASK QUESTION.

IT IS AN AUTHENTIC TO ASK QUESTION.

IT IS BRILLIANCE TO ASK QUESTION.

IT IS BRILLIANT TO ASK QUESTION.

IT IS BLISS ON TAP TO ASK QUESTION.

IT IS BEYOND FABULOUS TO ASK QUESTION.

IT IS BIOPHILIA TO ASK QUESTION.

IT IS BRIGHT TO ASK QUESTION.

IT IS BRIGHTEN TO ASK QUESTION.

IT IS BRIGHTNESS TO ASK QUESTION.

IT IS BALISTIC TO ASK QUESTION.

IT IS BLASTING TO ASK QUESTION.

IT IS AN ABLAZING TO ASK QUESTION.

IT IS AN BLINDING TO ASK QUESTION.

IT IS AN BREATHTAKING TO ASK QUESTION.

IT IS BUBBLING TO ASK QUESTION.

IT IS BUSTING TO ASK QUESTION.

IT IS BLISSCIPLINE COMPASSION TO ASK QUESTION.

IT IS COMPASSIONATE TO ASK QUESTION.

IT IS COMPETENT TO ASK QUESTION.

IT IS COMPETENCE TO ASK QUESTION.

IT IS COMPETENCY TO ASK QUESTION.

IT IS CONCENTRATION TO ASK QUESTION.

IT IS CONFIDENT TO ASK QUESTION.

IT IS CONFIDENCE TO ASK QUESTION.

IT IS CONSCIOUSNESS TO ASK QUESTION.

IT IS CONSISTENCY TO ASK QUESTION.

IT IS CONSISTENT TO ASK QUESTION.

IT IS CONTENT TO ASK QUESTION.

IT IS CONTENTMENT TO ASK QUESTION.

IT IS CONTINUITY TO ASK QUESTION.

IT IS CONTINUOUS TO ASK QUESTION.

IT IS CONTRIBUTION TO ASK QUESTION.

IT IS CONVICTION TO ASK QUESTION.

IT IS CONVINCING TO ASK QUESTION.

IT IS DARING TO ASK QUESTION.

IT IS DECISIVENESS TO ASK QUESTION.

IT IS DELIGHT TO ASK QUESTION.

IT IS DELIGHTED TO ASK QUESTION.

IT IS DELIGHTFUL TO ASK QUESTION.

IT IS DEPENDABILITY TO ASK QUESTION.

IT IS DESIRE TO ASK QUESTION.

IT IS DETERMINATION TO ASK QUESTION.

IT IS DEVOTION TO ASK QUESTION.

IT IS DIGNITY TO ASK QUESTION.

IT IS DILIGENCE TO ASK QUESTION.

IT IS DISCIPLINE TO ASK QUESTION.

IT IS DISCOVERY TO ASK QUESTION.

IT IS DISCRETION TO ASK QUESTION.

IT IS DIVERSITY TO ASK QUESTION.

IT IS EQUALITY TO ASK QUESTION.

IT IS EXCELLENCE TO ASK QUESTION.

IT IS EXCELLENT TO ASK QUESTION.

IT IS EXCITE TO ASK QUESTION.

IT IS EXCITEMENT TO ASK QUESTION.

IT IS EXCITED TO ASK QUESTION.

IT IS EXPERIENCE TO ASK QUESTION.

IT IS EXPERTISE TO ASK QUESTION.

IT IS EXPLORATION TO ASK QUESTION.

IT IS EXPRESSIVENESS TO ASK QUESTION.

IT IS EXPRESSING TO ASK QUESTION.

IT IS ENLIGHTENMENT TO ASK QUESTION.

IT IS ENLIGHTENED TO ASK QUESTION.

IT IS ETERNAL TO ASK QUESTION.

IT IS EXALTATION TO ASK QUESTION.

IT IS EMULATE TO ASK QUESTION.

IT IS EMPOWER TO ASK QUESTION.

IT IS EMPOWERING TO ASK QUESTION.

IT IS EMPOWERED TO ASK QUESTION.

IT IS EXPANSIVE TO ASK QUESTION.

IT IS EXHILARATING TO ASK QUESTION.

IT IS ENTHUSIASTIC TO ASK QUESTION.

IT IS ENTHUSIASM TO ASK QUESTION.

IT IS ENGROSSED TO ASK QUESTION.

IT IS ENCHANTED TO ASK QUESTION.

IT IS ENTRANCED TO ASK QUESTION.

IT IS ECSTATIC TO ASK QUESTION.

IT IS ELATED TO ASK QUESTION.

IT IS ENTHRALLED TO ASK QUESTION.

IT IS FORGIVENESS TO ASK QUESTION.

IT IS FORTITUDE TO ASK QUESTION.

IT IS FREE TO ASK QUESTION.

IT IS FREEDOM TO ASK QUESTION.

IT IS FRUGALITY TO ASK QUESTION.

IT IS FUN TO ASK QUESTION.

IT IS FUTURE TO ASK QUESTION.

IT IS FRIEND TO ASK QUESTION.

IT IS FRIENDLY TO ASK QUESTION.

IT IS FRIENDSHIP TO ASK QUESTION.

IT IS FRIENDLINESS TO ASK QUESTION.

IT IS FASCINATE TO ASK QUESTION.

IT IS FASCINATED TO ASK QUESTION.

IT IS FULFILL TO ASK QUESTION.

IT IS FULFILLED TO ASK QUESTION.

IT IS FEISTY TO ASK QUESTION.

IT IS FEISTINESS TO ASK QUESTION.

IT IS FEASIBLE TO ASK QUESTION.

Questions You May Ask

WHO IS ABLE?

WHO IS ACCEPT?

WHO IS ACCEPTANCE?

WHO IS ACCEPTABLE?

WHO IS ACCEPTED?

WHO IS ACCEPTING?

WHO IS ACTION?

WHO IS ACTIVATE?

WHO IS ACTIVE?

WHO IS ADD?

WHO IS ADDITION?

WHO IS ADORABLE?

WHO IS ADVANTAGE?

WHO IS AFFIRM?

WHO IS AGELESS?

WHO IS AGREE?

WHO IS AGREEABLE?

WHO IS AID?

WHO IS AIM?

WHO IS ABUNDANCE?

WHO IS ACCOUNTABILITY?

WHO IS ACCOMPLISHMENT?

WHO IS ACCOMPLISH?

WHO IS ACCURACY?

WHO IS ACHIEVEMENT?

WHO IS ACHIEVE?

WHO IS ACKNOWLEDGEMENT?

WHO IS ADAPTABILITY?

WHO IS ADVENTURE?

WHO IS ADVENTUROUS?

WHO IS AGILITY?

WHO IS ALERTNESS?

WHO IS AMBITION?

WHO IS ANTICIPATION?

WHO IS APPRECIATE?

Matumayini Lilia Mboleza

WHO IS APPRECIATION?

WHO IS APPRECIATIVE?

WHO IS APPRECIATIVENESS?

WHO IS ASSERTIVENESS?

WHO IS ASSERTIVE?

WHO IS ATTENTIVENESS?

WHO IS AUDACITY?

WHO IS AWARE?

WHO IS AWARENESS?

WHO IS AUTHENTIC?

WHO IS AUTHENTICITY?

WHO IS ABRACADABRA?

WHO IS ATTRACTION?

WHO IS ALLOW?

WHO IS ALLOWING?

WHO IS AFFECTION?

WHO IS AFFECTIONATE?

WHO IS ABSORBED?

WHO IS ALERT?

WHO IS AMAZED?

WHO IS AWE?

WHO IS AWED?

WHO IS ANIMATE?

WHO IS ANIMATED?

WHO IS ANIMATING?

WHO IS ANIMATION?

WHO IS ANIMATENESS?

WHO IS ARDENT?

WHO IS AMAZING?

WHO IS AWESOME?

WHO IS AWESOMENESS?

WHO IS AROUSED?

WHO IS ASTONISHED?

WHO IS ASTONISHING?

WHO IS AMUSED?

WHO IS AIR?

WHO IS AIRNESS?

WHO IS ALOHA?

WHO IS ADORE?

WHO IS ADMIRE?

WHO IS ADMIRABLE?

WHO IS ALLURE?

WHO IS ANGEL?

WHO IS ANGELIC?

WHO IS ALTRUISM?

WHO IS ALTRUISTIC?

WHO IS ABOUND?

WHO IS ABOUNDING?

WHO IS ABOUNDS?

WHO IS ABUNDANT?

WHO IS ABSOLUTE?

WHO IS ABSOLUTELY?

WHO IS ACCESSIBLE?

WHO IS ACCLAIMED?

WHO IS ACCOMMODATE?

WHO IS ACCOMMODATED?

WHO IS ACCOMMODATION?

WHO IS ACCOMMODATING?

WHO IS AMPLE?

WHO IS APPRECIATIVE JOY?

WHO IS AMIN?

WHO IS ACCENTUACTIVITY?

WHO IS ACTABILITY?

WHO IS AFFABLE?

WHO IS ALACRITY?

WHO IS ALTRUCAUSE?

WHO IS AMIABLE?

WHO IS ASTOUNDING?

WHO IS ATTRACTIVE?

WHO IS ALIVE?

WHO IS ALIVENESS?

WHO IS ACCLAIM?

WHO IS ABUNDANT GRATIFICATION?

WHO IS ACCLAMATION?

WHO IS ACCOMPLISHED?

WHO IS ACCOMPLISHMENTS?

Matumayini Lilia Mboleza

WHO IS ACCURATE?

WHO IS ACCURATELY?

WHO IS ACHIEVABLE?

WHO IS ACHIEVEMENTS?

WHO IS ACTION FOR HAPPINESS?

WHO IS ACTIVE AND CONSTRUCTIVE STEPS? WHO IS ACTS OF KINDNESS?

WHO IS ADAPTABLE?

WHO IS ADAPTIVE?

WHO IS ADEQUATE?

WHO IS ADMIRABLY?

WHO IS ADMIRATION?

WHO IS ADMIRED?

WHO IS ADORED?

WHO IS ADORING?

WHO IS ADORINGLY?

WHO IS ADVANCED?

WHO IS ADVANTAGEOUS?

WHO IS ADVANTAGEOUSLY?

WHO IS ADVANTAGES?

WHO IS AFFABILITY?

WHO IS AFFABLY?

WHO IS AFFINITY?

WHO IS AFFIRMATION?

WHO IS AFFIRMATIVE?

WHO IS AFFLUENCE?

WHO IS AFFLUENT?

WHO IS AFFORD?

WHO IS AFFORDABLE?

WHO IS AFFORDABLY?

WHO IS AGILE?

WHO IS AGILELY?

WHO IS AGREEABLENESS?

WHO IS AGREEABLY?

WHO IS ALIGNED?

WHO IS ALL IS WELL?

WHO IS ALLURING?

WHO IS ALLURINGLY?

WHO IS ALTERNATIVE HEALING?

WHO IS ALTRUISTICALLY?

WHO IS AMAZE?

WHO IS AMAZEMENT?

WHO IS AMAZES?

WHO IS AMAZINGLY?

WHO IS AMIABILITY?

WHO IS AMICABILITY?

WHO IS AMICABLE?

WHO IS AMICABLY?

WHO IS AMUSING?

WHO IS APPEAL?

WHO IS APPEALING?

WHO IS APPLAUD?

WHO IS APPRECIABLE?

WHO IS APPRECIATED?

WHO IS APPRECIATES?

WHO IS APPRECIATION OF BEAUTY?

WHO IS APPRECIATIVELY?

WHO IS APPROPRIATE?

WHO IS APPROVAL?

WHO IS APPROVE?

WHO IS ARDOR?

WHO IS ART OF APPRECIATION?

WHO IS ART OF STILLNESS?

WHO IS ART OF WELL-BEING?

WHO IS ASSURANCE?

WHO IS A REASON FOR BEING?

WHO IS ACARONAR?

WHO IS ACCOMMODATIVE?

WHO IS ALTITUDINARIAN?

WHO IS AMAZING WORDS?

WHO IS AMIABLY?

WHO IS ACCOLADE?

WHO IS ACUMEN?

WHO IS ADJUSTABLE?

WHO IS ADMIRER?

WHO IS ADMIRING?

WHO IS ADMIRINGLY?

WHO IS ADORER?

WHO IS ADROIT?

WHO IS ADROITLY?

WHO IS ADULATED?

WHO IS ADULATION?

WHO IS ADULATORY?

WHO IS ADVENTURESOME?

WHO IS ADVOCATED?

WHO IS AMBITIOUS?

WHO IS AMBITIOUSLY?

WHO IS AMELIORATE?

WHO IS AMENITY?

WHO IS AMITY?

WHO IS AMPLY?

WHO IS AMUSE?

WHO IS AMUSINGLY?

WHO IS APOTHEOSIS?

WHO IS ASSUME YOUR OWN VALUE?

WHO IS ASTONISHINGLY?

WHO IS ASTONISHMENT?

WHO IS ATTRIBUTIONAL STYLE QUESTIONNAIRE (ASQ)?

WHO IS AUTHENTIC HAPPINESS?

WHO IS AWAKEN?

WHO IS AWAKENING?

WHO IS AWE-GASMIC?

WHO IS AKASHIC RECORDS?

WHO IS AURORA?

WHO IS BEATIFY?

WHO IS BEATITUDE?

WHO IS BENEFICIAL?

WHO IS BENEFIT?

WHO IS BENEVOLENT?

WHO IS BELOVED?

WHO IS BEST?

WHO IS BETTER?

WHO IS BLESS?

WHO IS BLESSING?

WHO IS BLESSED?

WHO IS BLISS?

WHO IS BLISSFULNESS?

WHO IS BLISSFUL?

WHO IS BLOOM?

WHO IS BLOSSOM?

WHO IS BALANCE?

WHO IS BALANCED?

WHO IS BEAUTY?

WHO IS BEAUTIFUL?

WHO IS BEAUTIFULLY?

WHO IS BELONG?

WHO IS BELONGING?

WHO IS BOLDNESS?

WHO IS BRAVERY?

WHO IS BRILLIANCE?

WHO IS BRILLIANT?

WHO IS BLISS ON TAP?

WHO IS BEYOND FABULOUS?

WHO IS BIOPHILIA?

WHO IS BRIGHT?

WHO IS BRIGHTEN?

WHO IS BRIGHTNESS?

WHO IS BALISTIC?

WHO IS BLASTING?

WHO IS BLAZING?

WHO IS BLINDING?

WHO IS BREATHTAKING?

WHO IS BUBBLING?

WHO IS BUSTING?

WHO IS BLISSCIPLINE?

WHO IS BUYANCY?

WHO IS BULLISHNESS?

WHO IS BRISKNESS?

WHO IS BUOYANCY?

WHO IS BREEZINESS?

WHO IS BRIO?

WHO IS BE EXTRAORDINARY?

Matumayini Lilia Mboleza

WHO IS BE HAPPY?

WHO IS BEAUTIFY?

WHO IS BEING AT REST?

WHO IS BENEFACTOR?

WHO IS BENEFITS?

WHO IS BENEVOLENCE?

WHO IS BENEVOLENTLY?

WHO IS BENEVOLENTLY CHEERFUL STATE OF MIND?

WHO IS BEST OF ALL POSSIBLE WORLDS?

WHO IS BEYOND?

WHO IS BEAUTY IN ALL THINGS?

WHO IS WHO IS BEINGNESS?

WHO IS BELIEVABLE?

WHO IS BLOOD-BROTHERS?

WHO IS BOHEMIAN SOUL?

WHO IS BOHO-SOUL?

WHO IS BADASSERY?

WHO IS BEST-SELLING?

WHO IS BETTER AND BETTER?

WHO IS BETTER-KNOWN?

WHO IS BETTER-THAN-EXPECTED?

WHO IS BEYOND THANK YOU?

WHO IS BIG VISION?

WHO IS BLITHESOME?

WHO IS BLOSSOMING?

WHO IS BONUS?

WHO IS BLING BLING?

WHO IS BUDO?

WHO IS BLASTING LOVE?

WHO IS BUDDHAHOOD?

WHO IS CARE?

WHO IS CARING?

WHO IS CALM?

WHO IS CREATE?

WHO IS CREATIVE?

WHO IS CREATIVITY?

WHO IS CREATIVENESS?

WHO IS CAPABLE?

WHO IS CAPABILITY?

WHO IS CAPABLY?

WHO IS CELEBRATE?

WHO IS CELEBRATION?

WHO IS CERTAIN?

WHO IS CERTAINTY?

WHO IS CHARITABLE?

WHO IS CHARITY?

WHO IS CHARM?

WHO IS CHARMING?

WHO IS CHARMER?

WHO IS CHOICE?

WHO IS CLEAN?

WHO IS CLEANLINESS?

WHO IS COMFORT?

WHO IS COMFORTABLE?

WHO IS COMFORTING?

WHO IS CUDDLE?

WHO IS CUDDLING?

WHO IS CANDOR?

WHO IS CAREFULNESS?

WHO IS CHALLENGE?

WHO IS CHANGE?

WHO IS CHEERFUL?

WHO IS CHEERFULNESS?

WHO IS CLARITY?

WHO IS COLLABORATION?

WHO IS COMMITMENT?

WHO IS COMMUNICATION?

WHO IS COMMUNITY?

WHO IS COMPASSION?

WHO IS COMPASSIONATE?

WHO IS COMPETENT?

WHO IS COMPETENCE?

WHO IS COMPETENCY?

WHO IS CONCENTRATION?

WHO IS CONFIDENT?

WHO IS CONFIDENCE?

Matumayini Lilia Mboleza

WHO IS CONSCIOUSNESS?

WHO IS CONSISTENCY?

WHO IS CONSISTENT?

WHO IS CONTENT?

WHO IS CONTENTMENT?

WHO IS CONTINUITY?

WHO IS CONTINUOUS?

WHO IS CONTRIBUTION?

WHO IS CONVICTION?

WHO IS CONVINCING?

WHO IS COOPERATION?

WHO IS COURAGE?

WHO IS COURTESY?

WHO IS COURTEOUS?

WHO IS CURIOUS?

WHO IS CURIOSITY?

WHO IS CHAKRA?

WHO IS COOL?

WHO IS CLEAR HEADED?

WHO IS CENTERED?

WHO IS CLOSENESS?

WHO IS COMPANIONSHIP?

WHO IS CONSIDERATE?

WHO IS CONSIDERATION?

WHO IS COMMUNION?

WHO IS CONNECT?

WHO IS CONNECTED?

WHO IS CONNECTION?

WHO IS CONNECTEDNESS?

WHO IS CONQUER?

WHO IS CUTE?

WHO IS CHARISMA?

WHO IS CHARISMATIC?

WHO IS COLLECTED?

WHO IS CHEERFUL WILLINGNESS?

WHO IS CHEERS?

WHO IS CONGRUENCE?

WHO IS CORDIAL?

WHO IS CRANK (UP)?

WHO IS CAPITAL?

WHO IS CORKING?

WHO IS CLEAR?

WHO IS CARESS?

WHO IS CHEERFUL MOOD?

WHO IS COMPLIMENTARY WORDS?

WHO IS CONTENTED?

WHO IS COZINESS?

WHO IS CUTENESS?

WHO IS CAREFREENESS?

WHO IS CAREFREE?

WHO IS CENTERING?

WHO IS CENTERING MEDITATION?

WHO IS CITIZEN OF MASTERY?

WHO IS CO-CREATING?

WHO IS CO-CREATOR?

WHO IS COHESION?

WHO IS CONTINUAL STREAM OF SYNCHRONICITY?

WHO IS CREATIVE PROCESS?

WHO IS CREATIVE AFFIRMATIONS?

WHO IS COMPOSTURE?

WHO IS CONCORD?

WHO IS CEREBRO?

WHO IS CONSCIOUSNESS ENGINEERING? WHO IS CHI?

WHO IS CLASSY?

WHO IS COPACABANA?

WHO IS COSMIC AWARENESS DIRECTION?

WHO IS DELICATE?

WHO IS DECENT?

WHO IS DESIRABLE?

WHO IS DELICIOUS?

WHO IS DELICIOUSNESS?

WHO IS DO

WHO IS DREAM?

WHO IS DREAMY?

WHO IS DYNAMIC?

WHO IS DARING?

WHO IS DECISIVENESS?

WHO IS DELIGHT?

WHO IS DELIGHTED?

WHO IS DELIGHTFUL?

WHO IS DEPENDABILITY?

WHO IS DESIRE?

WHO IS DETERMINATION?

WHO IS DEVOTION?

WHO IS DIGNITY?

WHO IS DILIGENCE?

WHO IS DISCIPLINE?

WHO IS DISCOVERY?

WHO IS DISCRETION?

WHO IS DIVERSITY?

WHO IS DRIVE?

WHO IS DUTY?

WHO IS DIVINE?

WHO IS DAZZLED?

WHO IS DISNEY?

WHO IS DEVOTED?

WHO IS DANDY?

WHO IS DAIMON?

WHO IS DEBONAIR?

WHO IS DETACHMENT?

WHO IS DEDICATED?

WHO IS DAUWTRAPPEN?

WHO IS DAZZLE?

WHO IS DELIGHTFULLY?

WHO IS DEFENCELESSNESS?

WHO IS DEEPER PART OF YOU?

WHO IS DESERVE?

WHO IS DESERVEDNESS?

WHO IS DESERVINGNESS?

WHO IS DIS-IDENTIFY?

WHO IS DOPE?

WHO IS DOPE CHILL OUT?

WHO IS EMPATHY?

WHO IS EMPATHIZE?

WHO IS EMPHATIC?

WHO IS EASY?

WHO IS EASILY?

WHO IS EASIER?

WHO IS EDUCATE?

WHO IS EDUCATION?

WHO IS EDUCATED?

WHO IS EFFICIENT?

WHO IS ENABLE?

WHO IS ENABLED?

WHO IS ENERGETIC?

WHO IS ENERGIZE?

WHO IS ENERGY?

WHO IS ENGAGE?

WHO IS ENGAGING?

WHO IS ENGAGED?

WHO IS ENJOY?

WHO IS ENJOYMENT?

WHO IS ENOUGH?

WHO IS EAGER?

WHO IS EAGERNESS?

WHO IS EFFECTIVENESS?

WHO IS EFFICIENCY?

WHO IS ELATION?

WHO IS ELEGANCE?

WHO IS ENCOURAGE?

WHO IS ENCOURAGEMENT?

WHO IS ENCOURAGED?

WHO IS ENDURANCE?

WHO IS EQUALITY?

WHO IS EXCELLENCE?

WHO IS EXCELLENT?

WHO IS EXCITE?

WHO IS EXCITEMENT?

WHO IS EXCITED?

WHO IS EXPERIENCE?

WHO IS EXPERTISE?

WHO IS EXPLORATION?

Matumayini Lilia Mboleza

WHO IS EXPRESSIVENESS?

WHO IS EXPRESSING?

WHO IS ENLIGHTENMENT?

WHO IS ENLIGHTENED?

WHO IS ETERNAL?

WHO IS EXALTATION?

WHO IS EMULATE?

WHO IS EMPOWER?

WHO IS EMPOWERING?

WHO IS EMPOWERED?

WHO IS EXPANSIVE?

WHO IS EXHILARATING?

WHO IS ENTHUSIASTIC?

WHO IS ENTHUSIASM?

WHO IS ENGROSSED?

WHO IS ENCHANTED?

WHO IS ENTRANCED?

WHO IS ECSTATIC?

WHO IS ELATED?

WHO IS ENTHRALLED?

WHO IS EXUBERANT?

WHO IS EXUBERANCE?

WHO IS EXPECTANT?

WHO IS EQUANIMOUS?

WHO IS ENLIVENED?

WHO IS EFFICACY?

WHO IS EASE?

WHO IS EXEMPLARY?

WHO IS EXTRAORDINARY?

WHO IS EARNEST?

WHO IS ELEVATE?

WHO IS ELEVATED?

WHO IS EQUANIMITY?

WHO IS EASE-OF-MIND?

WHO IS EXCITED ANTICIPATION?

WHO IS EXTRA?

WHO IS EQUITY?

WHO IS EQUITABLY?

Matumayini Lilia Mboleza

WHO IS EQUITABLE?

WHO IS EASY TO TALK TO?

WHO IS EASY TO APPROACH?

WHO IS ECSTATIFY?

WHO IS EUDAEMONISM?

WHO IS EUDAEMONIST?

WHO IS EUDAEMONISTIC?

WHO IS EUDAIMONIA?

WHO IS EUDAMONIA?

WHO IS EVOLVE?

WHO IS EXALTING?

WHO IS EXSTATISFY?,

WHO IS EXULTANT?

WHO IS ASTRONOMICAL?

WHO IS CHAMPION?

WHO IS CHAMP?

WHO IS ELECTRIC?

WHO IS ENORMOUS?

WHO IS EXCEPTIONAL?

WHO IS EXCITING?

WHO IS EXQUISITE?

WHO IS EFFORTLESSNESS?

WHO IS EUNOIA?

WHO IS ECOSOPHY?

WHO IS EBULLIENCE?

WHO IS EMBRACE?

WHO IS EMPOWERING WORDS?

WHO IS ENCOURAGING WORDS?

WHO IS ERLEBNIS?

WHO IS EFFORTLESS EASE?

WHO IS EFFORTLESSLY?

WHO IS EKAGGATA?

WHO IS EMBODY THE LOVE?

WHO IS EARTHING?

WHO IS EVER-JOYOUS?

WHO IS EVER-JOYOUS NOW?

WHO IS ETHEREAL?

WHO IS ENDLESS?

WHO IS E MA HO?

WHO IS FANTASTIC?

WHO IS FEEL GOOD?

WHO IS FEELING GOOD?

WHO IS FLOW?

WHO IS FLOWING?

WHO IS FABULOUS?

WHO IS FAIR?

WHO IS FAITH?

WHO IS FAITHFUL?

WHO IS FAME?

WHO IS FAVORITE?

WHO IS FAIRNESS?

WHO IS FAMILY?

WHO IS FIDELITY?

WHO IS FLEXIBILITY?

WHO IS FOCUS?

WHO IS FLOURISH?

WHO IS FORGIVE?

WHO IS FORGIVING?

WHO IS FORGIVENESS?

WHO IS FORTITUDE?

WHO IS FREE?

WHO IS FREEDOM?

WHO IS FRUGALITY?

WHO IS FUN?

WHO IS FUTURE?

WHO IS FRIEND?

WHO IS FRIENDLY?

WHO IS FRIENDSHIP?

WHO IS FRIENDLINESS?

WHO IS FASCINATE?

WHO IS FASCINATED?

WHO IS FULFILL?

WHO IS FULFILLED?

WHO IS FOOD?

WHO IS FEISTY?

WHO IS FEISTINESS?

WHO IS FEASIBLE?

WHO IS FINE?

WHO IS FEARLESS?

WHO IS FESTIVE?

WHO IS FESTIVENESS?

WHO IS FIT?

WHO IS FANTABULOUS?

WHO IS FREECYCLE?

WHO IS FUNERIFIC?

WHO IS FUNOLOGY?

WHO IS FLAWLESS?

WHO IS FAMOUS?

WHO IS FANCY?

WHO IS FLASHY?

WHO IS FTW?

WHO IS FUNNY JOKES?

WHO IS FLAUNTING?

WHO IS FONDLE?

WHO IS FRIC-TIONLESSLY?

WHO IS FLAWLESSLY?

WHO IS FLOURISHING?

WHO IS FORTUITOUS?

WHO IS FUN-LOVING?

WHO IS FREE-SPIRITED?

WHO IS FELICITY?

WHO IS GLOW?

WHO IS GENEROUS?

WHO IS GENEROSITY?

WHO IS GENERATE?

WHO IS GENIAL?

WHO IS GENIUS?

WHO IS GENUINE?

WHO IS GIFT?

WHO IS GIVE?

WHO IS GIVING?

WHO IS GOOD?

WHO IS GOODNESS?

WHO IS GOING THE EXTRA MILE?,

WHO IS GRACE?

WHO IS GRATITUDE?

WHO IS GRATEFULNESS?

WHO IS GROW?

WHO IS GROWTH?

WHO IS GUIDE?

WHO IS GUIDING?

WHO IS GUIDANCE?

WHO IS GOD?

WHO IS GROUNDED?

WHO IS GLORY?

WHO IS GODLINESS?

WHO IS GOOD-FEELING?

WHO IS GROOVY?

WHO IS GIDDY?

WHO IS GLAD?

WHO IS GOOD HEALTH?

WHO IS GLAMOR?

WHO IS GIGGLING?

WHO IS GODDESS?

WHO IS GORGEOUS?

WHO IS GORGEOUSNESS?

WHO IS GRANDIOSITY?

WHO IS GENERAVITY?

WHO IS GENTLEMAN?

WHO IS GARGANTUAN?

WHO IS GRAND?

WHO IS GREAT?

WHO IS GINGER?

WHO IS GOOD-HUMORED?

WHO IS GOODWILL?

WHO IS GREATFUL?

WHO IS GEMUTLICHKEIT?

WHO IS GIBIGIANA?

WHO IS GIGIL?

WHO IS GOOD INDWELLING SPIRIT?

WHO IS GOOD WORD?

WHO IS GOOD WORDS?

WHO IS GOOD-HUMORED?

WHO IS GOODWILL?

WHO IS GOOD FORTUNE?

WHO IS GYPSY SOUL?

WHO IS GAME-CHANGER?

WHO IS GENERATOR OF LIFE?

WHO IS GRACEFULLY?

WHO IS GRACIOUSNESS?

WHO IS GOLDILOCKS?

WHO IS GENUINENESS?

WHO IS GREAT ZEAL?

WHO IS GOOD DONE IN SECRET?

WHO IS HOPE?

WHO IS HOPEFULNESS?

WHO IS HAPPINESS?

WHO IS HAPPY?

WHO IS HAPPILY?

WHO IS HARMONIOUS?

WHO IS HARMONIZE?

WHO IS HARMONY?

WHO IS HEALTH?

WHO IS HEALTHY?

WHO IS HEART?

WHO IS HELLO?

WHO IS HELP?

WHO IS HELPFUL?

WHO IS HELPING?

WHO IS HOT?

WHO IS HONEST?

WHO IS HONESTY?

WHO IS HUMAN?

WHO IS HUMOR?

WHO IS HELPFULNESS?

WHO IS HERO?

WHO IS HEROISM?

WHO IS HOLY?

WHO IS HOLINESS?

WHO IS HONOR?

WHO IS HOSPITALITY?

WHO IS HUMBLE?

WHO IS HEAVEN?

WHO IS HEAVENLY?

WHO IS HALO?

WHO IS HEARTFELT?

WHO IS HEARTWARMING?

WHO IS ONE-POINTEDNESS?

WHO IS HAPPY HEARTED?

WHO IS HEEDFUL?

WHO IS HANDSOME?

WHO IS HUGE?

WHO IS HIGH-SPIRITEDNESS?

WHO IS HIGHLY DISTINGUISHED?

WHO IS HAPPY WORDS?

WHO IS HEART-OPENING?

WHO IS HOSPITABLE?

WHO IS HUMAN FLOURISHING?

WHO IS HIGHLY DISTINGUISHED?

WHO IS HARNESS?

WHO IS HEIGHTENED?

WHO IS HOLISTIC?

WHO IS HOLY SPIRIT?

WHO IS HALL OF AWESOMENESS?

WHO IS HONEY BADGER?

WHO IS HIGHER CONSCIOUSNESS?

WHO IS HALYCON?

WHO IS HABITUATION?

WHO IS HAKUNA MATATA?

WHO IS IMAGINATION?

WHO IS INSPIRE?

WHO IS INSPIRATION?

WHO IS INSPIRED?

WHO IS INSPIRATIONAL?

WHO IS IN-LOVE?

WHO IS IDEA?

WHO IS INCREDIBLE?

WHO IS INNOVATE?

WHO IS INNOVATION?

WHO IS INTERESTING?

WHO IS INTEREST?

WHO IS INTERESTED?

WHO IS IMPROVEMENT?

WHO IS INDEPENDENCE?

WHO IS INFLUENCE?

WHO IS INGENUITY?

WHO IS INNER PEACE?

WHO IS INSIGHT?

WHO IS INSIGHTFULNESS?

WHO IS INSIGHTFUL?

WHO IS INTEGRITY?

WHO IS INTELLIGENCE?

WHO IS INTELLIGENT?

WHO IS INTENSITY?

WHO IS INTIMACY?

WHO IS INTUITIVENESS?

WHO IS INVENTIVENESS?

WHO IS INVESTING?

WHO IS INTENTION?

WHO IS INVIGORATE?

WHO IS INVIGORATED?

WHO IS INTRIGUED?

WHO IS INVOLVE?

WHO IS INVOLVED?

WHO IS INCLUSION?

WHO IS INNOCENT?

WHO IS INEFFABLE?

WHO IS INEFFABILITY?

WHO IS INTREPID?

WHO IS IDEALISM?

WHO IS ILLUMINATION?

WHO IS ILLUMINATED?

WHO IS INCOMPARABLE?

WHO IS INVINCIBLE?

WHO IS INQUISITIVE?

WHO IS INFINITE?

WHO IS INFINITY?

WHO IS ILLUSTRIOUS?

WHO IS INNER?

WHO IS ICHARIBA CHODE?

WHO IS IKIGAI?

WHO IS INCREDIBLE CUTENESS?

WHO IS INDWELLING?

WHO IS INSPIRATIONAL WORDS?

WHO IS INSPIRING WORD?

WHO IS INSPIRING WORDS?

WHO IS IRIDESCENT?

WHO IS ILLUSTRIOUS?

WHO IS INNER?

WHO IS INNER SPIRIT?

WHO IS INTERCONNECTED?

WHO IS INTERCONNECTIVITY?

WHO IS INTUITION?

WHO IS INCLUSIVENESS?

WHO IS JOY?

WHO IS JOYFUL?

WHO IS JOYOUS?

WHO IS JOKE?

WHO IS JOLLY?

WHO IS JOVIAL?

WHO IS JUST?

WHO IS JUSTICE?

WHO IS JUBILANT?

WHO IS JUVENESCENT?

WHO IS JUMPY?

WHO IS JAMMIN?

WHO IS JUBILINGO?

WHO IS KINDNESS?

WHO IS KIND?

WHO IS KIND-HEART?

WHO IS KINDLY?

WHO IS KEEP-UP?

WHO IS KISS?

WHO IS KNOWLEDGE?

WHO IS KITTENS?

WHO IS KEEN?

WHO IS KAAJHUAB?

WHO IS KALON?

WHO IS KILIG?

WHO IS KIND WORDS?

WHO IS KOIBITO KIBUN?

WHO IS KI?

WHO IS KALEIDOSCOPES OF BUTTERFLIES?

WHO IS LIKE?

WHO IS LAUGH?

WHO IS LAUGHING?

WHO IS LEARN?

WHO IS LEARNING?

WHO IS LIFE?

WHO IS LIVE?

WHO IS LIVING?

WHO IS LUXURY?

WHO IS LONGEVITY?

WHO IS LOYALTY?

WHO IS LOYAL?

WHO IS LOVE?

WHO IS LOVABLE?

WHO IS LOVING?

WHO IS LIBERTY?

WHO IS LOGIC?

WHO IS LEADER?

WHO IS LEADERSHIP?

WHO IS LUCK?

WHO IS LUCKY?

WHO IS LIGHT?

WHO IS LOVING-KINDNESS?

WHO IS LIVELY?

WHO IS LIFE OF THE PARTY?

WHO IS LOVELY?

WHO IS LOVING ACCEPTANCE?

WHO IS LOVING FEELINGS?

WHO IS LIGHTWORKER?

WHO IS LEADING?

WHO IS LIGHT FOG?

WHO IS LIVES THROUGH?

LOVE WORDS?

WHO IS LOVER OF BEAUTY?

WHO IS LUSTROUS?

WHO IS LUSTROUS COLORS?

WHO IS LIGHT-HEARTED?

WHO IS LEEWAY?

WHO IS LET GO?

WHO IS LETTING GO?

WHO IS LIVELINESS?

WHO IS LOVE FULFILLED?

WHO IS LOVING ATTENTION?

WHO IS MEANING?

WHO IS MEANINGFUL?

WHO IS MORE?

WHO IS MAGNIFICENT?

WHO IS MAJESTY?

WHO IS MANY?

WHO IS MARVELOUS?

WHO IS MERIT?

WHO IS MOTIVATE?

WHO IS MIRACLE?

WHO IS MAGIC?

WHO IS MAKING A DIFFERENCE?

WHO IS MASTERY?

WHO IS MATURITY?

WHO IS MINDFUL?

WHO IS MINDFULNESS?

WHO IS MODESTY?

WHO IS MOTIVATION?

WHO IS MOTIVATIONAL?

WHO IS MERCY?

WHO IS MEDITATION?

WHO IS MIND-BLOWING?

WHO IS MELLOW?

WHO IS MOVED?

WHO IS MOVEMENT?

WHO IS MUTUALITY?

WHO IS MOURNING?

WHO IS MELIORISM?

WHO IS MENCH?

WHO IS MINDSIGHT?

WHO IS MINDSIGHT?

WHO IS MAJOR?

WHO IS MILD?

WHO IS MEANINGFUL WORDS?

WHO IS MEMORABLE?

WHO IS MORPHING?

WHO IS MOTIVATED WORDS?

WHO IS MOTIVATING WORDS?

WHO IS MOTIVATIONAL WORDS

MOVING?

WHO IS MAGNETIC TO LOVE?

WHO IS MIRTHFUL?

WHO IS MYRIAD?

WHO IS MOJO?

WHO IS NOBLE?

WHO IS NURTURING?

WHO IS NURTURE?

WHO IS NON-RESISTANCE?

WHO IS NON-RESISTANT?

WHO IS NEW?

WHO IS NICE?

WHO IS NIRVANA?

WHO IS NEAT?

WHO IS NATURE-MADE?

WHO IS NOURISH?

WHO IS NOURISHED?

WHO IS NOURISHING?

WHO IS NOURISHMENT?

WHO IS NAMASTE?

WHO IS NEOTENY?

WHO IS NICE WORDS?

WHO IS NOVATURIENT?

WHO IS NON-DUALITY?

WHO IS OPTIMIST?

WHO IS OPTIMISTIC?

WHO IS OUTSTANDING?

WHO IS OK?

WHO IS ON?

WHO IS ONWARDS?

WHO IS OPEN?

WHO IS OPENLY?

WHO IS OPENING?

WHO IS OPEN-MINDED?

WHO IS OPPORTUNITY?

WHO IS ORIGINAL?

WHO IS OPENNESS?

WHO IS OPTIMISM?

WHO IS ORDER?

WHO IS ORGANIZATION?

WHO IS ORIGINALITY?

WHO IS OUTCOME?

WHO IS ORIENTATION?

WHO IS OBEDIENT?

WHO IS OPEN HEARTED?

WHO IS OMG?

WHO IS OVERCOME?

WHO IS OM MANI PADME HUM?

WHO IS OUTGOING?

WHO IS ONENESS?

WHO IS OUTERNATIONALIST?

WHO IS OVERLY OPTIMISTIC?

WHO IS ORENDA?

WHO IS OWNING YOUR POWER?

WHO IS ONEUP?

WHO IS OMNISCIENCE?

WHO IS OKAGE SAMA?

WHO IS PERFECT?

WHO IS PERFECTION?

WHO IS POSITIVE ENERGY?

WHO IS POSITIVE THOUGHTS?

WHO IS POSITIVE EVENTS?

WHO IS POSITIVE CIRCUMSTANCES?

WHO IS POSITIVE BELIEFS?

WHO IS PEACE?

WHO IS PACIFY?

WHO IS PARADISE?

WHO IS PARADISIAC?

WHO IS PASSION?

WHO IS PASSIONATE?

WHO IS PLEASE?

WHO IS PURE?

WHO IS PERCEPTIVENESS?

WHO IS PERSEVERANCE?

WHO IS PERSISTENCE?

WHO IS PERSONAL GROWTH?

WHO IS PLEASURE?

WHO IS POSITIVE ATTITUDE?

WHO IS POSITIVE WORDS?

WHO IS POWER?

WHO IS POWERFUL?

WHO IS PRACTICALITY?

WHO IS PRECISION?

WHO IS PREPAREDNESS?

WHO IS PRESENCE?

WHO IS PRESERVATION?

WHO IS PRIVACY?

WHO IS PROACTIVITY?

WHO IS PROACTIVE?

WHO IS PROGRESS?

WHO IS PROSPERITY PROSPEROUS?

WHO IS PUNCTUALITY?

WHO IS PUNCTUAL?

WHO IS PATIENCE?

WHO IS PROUD?

WHO IS PLEASED?

WHO IS PLAY?

WHO IS PLAYFUL?

WHO IS PLAYFULNESS?

WHO IS PARTICIPATION?

WHO IS PURPOSE?

WHO IS PICK-ME-UP?

WHO IS PRONIA?

WHO IS PIOUS?

WHO IS PUPPIES?

WHO IS POLITE?

WHO IS POSITIVE MIND?

WHO IS POSITIVE THINKING?

WHO IS PRETTY?

WHO IS PRECIOUS?

WHO IS PARDON?

WHO IS PERKINESS?

WHO IS PIQUANCY?

WHO IS POSICHOICE?

WHO IS POSIDRIVING?

WHO IS POSIFIT?

WHO IS POSILENZ?

WHO IS POSIMASS?

WHO IS POSIMINDER?

WHO IS POSIRATIO?

WHO IS POSIRIPPLE?

WHO IS POSIRIPPLER?

WHO IS POSIRIPPLES?

WHO IS POSISINGER?

WHO IS POSISITE?

WHO IS POSISTRENGTH?

WHO IS POSITIBILITARIAN?

WHO IS POSITRACTION?

WHO IS POSITUDE?

WHO IS POSIVALUES?

WHO IS POSIWORD?

WHO IS POSSIBILITARIAN?

WHO IS PROMPTNESS?

WHO IS PROTO?

WHO IS PRICELESS?

WHO IS PEP?

WHO IS PEPPINESS?

WHO IS PERMALICIOUS?

WHO IS PLUCKY?

WHO IS POLLYANNAISM?

WHO IS PRIDE?

WHO IS POSITIVE FEELINGS?

WHO IS PEACE OF MIND?

WHO IS PEACEFUL WORDS?

WHO IS PETRICHOR?

WHO IS PHILOCALIST?

WHO IS POSITIVE EMOTIONS?

WHO IS POSITIVE FEELINGS?

WHO IS POSITIVE VOCABULARY?

WHO IS POWER WORDS?

WHO IS POWERFUL POSITIVE WORDS?

WHO IS POWERFUL WORDS?

WHO IS POWER-ON?

WHO IS POWER-UP?

WHO IS PROTECT?

WHO IS POLITENESS?

WHO IS POUR YOUR LOVE?

WHO IS POWERFUL POSSIBILITY?

WHO IS PRIVILEGE?

WHO IS PROPITIOUS?

WHO IS POSITIVE THESAURUS?

WHO IS POSITIVE ADJECTIVES?

WHO IS PICTURESQUE?

WHO IS PRANA?

WHO IS PANACHE?

WHO IS QUALITY?

WHO IS QUIET?

WHO IS QUIETNESS?

WHO IS QUAINT?

WHO IS QUIESCENT?

WHO IS QUEENLY?

WHO IS QUICKENING?

WHO IS QUIDDITY?

WHO IS QUIESCENT MIND?

WHO IS QUALITY WORDS?

WHO IS QUANTUMNESS?

WHO IS QUANTUM CONSCIOUSNESS?

WHO IS RESPECT?

WHO IS RADIANT?

WHO IS READY?

WHO IS READINESS?

WHO IS REAL?

WHO IS REALITY?

WHO IS REASON?

WHO IS RECOMMEND?

WHO IS REFRESH?

WHO IS REFRESHED?

WHO IS RELAX?

WHO IS RELAXED?

WHO IS RELIEF?

WHO IS RELIEVE?

WHO IS RELIEVED?

WHO IS REMARKABLE?

WHO IS RATIONALITY?

WHO IS RECOGNITION?

WHO IS RELATIONSHIPS?

WHO IS RELIABLE?

WHO IS RELIABILITY?

WHO IS RELIGION?

WHO IS RESOURCEFULNESS?

WHO IS RESPONSIBILITY?

WHO IS RIGHTEOUSNESS?

WHO IS RISK-TAKING?

WHO IS ROMANCE?

WHO IS REVELATION?

WHO IS REVIVED?

WHO IS RESTORE?

WHO IS RESTORED?

WHO IS REST?

WHO IS RESTED?

WHO IS RENEW?

WHO IS RENEWED?

WHO IS REJUVENATE?

Matumayini Lilia Mboleza

WHO IS REJUVENATED?

WHO IS RAPTURE?

WHO IS RAPTUROUS?

WHO IS RESILIENT?

WHO IS RESILIENCE?

WHO IS REVERENCE?

WHO IS RIPE?

WHO IS REBORN?

WHO IS RELATEDNESS?

WHO IS RASASVADA?

WHO IS REPOSE?

WHO IS ROSINESS?

WHO IS RELENT?

WHO IS RENOWNED?

WHO IS RESPECTED?

WHO IS RAINBOW?

WHO IS ROMANTIC?

WHO IS RELENT?

WHO IS RENOWNED?

WHO IS RADIATE?

WHO IS RECOGNIZE?

WHO IS RELEASING?

WHO IS RIGHTFUL?

WHO IS ROCKSTAR?

WHO IS SCOPE?

WHO IS SMILE?

WHO IS SMILING?

WHO IS SOULMATE?

WHO IS SOUL?

WHO IS SOULFUL?

WHO IS SACRED?

WHO IS SAFE?

WHO IS SAFETY?

WHO IS SECURE?

WHO IS SECURED?

WHO IS SECURITY?

WHO IS SUSTAIN?

WHO IS SUSTAINED?

WHO IS SAVE?

WHO IS SAVINGS?

WHO IS SIMPLE?

WHO IS SIMPLIFY?

WHO IS SELFLESSNESS?

WHO IS SELF-ESTEEM?

WHO IS SERVICE?

WHO IS SIMPLICITY?

WHO IS SINCERITY?

WHO IS SKILL?

WHO IS SKILLED?

WHO IS SPIRIT?

WHO IS SERENE?

WHO IS SERENITY?

WHO IS STABILITY?

WHO IS STRENGTH?

WHO IS STYLE?

WHO IS SYSTEMATIZATION?

WHO IS SELF-LOVE?

WHO IS STRIVE?

WHO IS SALVATION?

WHO IS SELF-RESPECT?

WHO IS SELF-FORGIVENESS?

WHO IS SERVE?

WHO IS SYMPATHETIC?

WHO IS SELF-COMPASSION?

WHO IS SELF-KINDNESS?

WHO IS SPELLBOUND?

WHO IS STIMULATED?

WHO IS STIMULATING?

WHO IS STIMULATION?

WHO IS SATISFIED?

WHO IS STILL?

WHO IS SURPRISED?

WHO IS SLEEP?

WHO IS SEXUAL EXPRESSION?

WHO IS SHELTER?

WHO IS SELF-EXPRESSION?

WHO IS SPACE?

WHO IS SPACIOUS?

WHO IS SPONTANEITY?

WHO IS SPONTANEOUS?

WHO IS SUNSHINE?

WHO IS SPARK?

WHO IS SPARKLE?

WHO IS SPARKLES?

WHO IS SWEET?

WHO IS SWEETNESS?

WHO IS SUPPORT?

WHO IS SUPPORTING?

WHO IS SUPPORTED?

WHO IS SEXY?

WHO IS SEXINESS?

WHO IS SUPREME?

WHO IS SUCCULENT?

WHO IS SWEETHEART?

WHO IS STUDY?

WHO IS STUDIOUS?

WHO IS SAVOUR?

WHO IS SAVOURING?

WHO IS SUFFICIENT?

WHO IS STUPENDOUS?

WHO IS SWAG?

WHO IS SWAGGY?

WHO IS SPLENDID?

WHO IS SMART?

WHO IS SPECTACULAR?

WHO IS SPECIAL?

WHO IS SERENDIPITY?

WHO IS SYNERGY?

WHO IS SHINE?

WHO IS SHINING?

WHO IS START?

WHO IS STEADFASTNESS?

WHO IS SUBLIME?

WHO IS SUNNINESS?

WHO IS SUPERPOWER?

WHO IS SPUNKY?

WHO IS SHAPE-SHIFTING VIRTUOSO?

WHO IS SOUL-STRETCHING?

WHO IS STRONG WORDS?

WHO IS SACRED SPACE?

WHO IS SHIFT IN FOCUS?

WHO IS SHOW UP MORE PRESENT?

WHO IS STELLAR?

WHO IS SUPERCHARGE?

WHO IS SUPERCHARGED?

WHO IS SYMPTOMS OF GREATNESS?

WHO IS SYNCHRONICITY?

WHO IS SASSY?

WHO IS SUPERCALIFRAGILISTIC?

WHO IS SUPERCALIFRAGILISTICEXPIALIDOCIOUS?

WHO IS SLAYING YOUR DRAGON?

WHO IS TRUE?

WHO IS TRUST?

WHO IS TRUSTING?

WHO IS TACT?

WHO IS TEACH?

WHO IS TEACHABLE?

WHO IS TEAM?

WHO IS THANKFUL?

WHO IS THANK?

WHO IS THANK-YOU?

WHO IS THANKFULNESS?

WHO IS THERAPY?

WHO IS TIME?

WHO IS TEAMWORK?

WHO IS TIMELINESS?

WHO IS TOLERANCE?

WHO IS TRADITION?

WHO IS TRANQUIL?

WHO IS TRANQUILITY?

WHO IS TRUTH?

WHO IS TRUTHFULNESS?

WHO IS TENDER?

WHO IS THRILLED?

WHO IS TOUCH?

WHO IS TOUCHED?

WHO IS TICKLED?

WHO IS TO MATTER?

WHO IS TO KNOW?

WHO IS TO BE KNOWN?

WHO IS TO BE SEEN?

WHO IS TRANSFORMATIVE?

WHO IS TRANSFORMATION?

WHO IS TRANSFORM?

WHO IS TRIUMPH?

WHO IS THRIVE?

WHO IS THRIVING?

WHO IS TENACITY?

WHO IS TO BE?

WHO IS TRANSPARENT?

WHO IS TEMUL?

WHO IS TENDERLY?

WHO IS TIDSOPTIMIST?

WHO IS TIME OPTIMIST?

WHO IS TO LET GO?

WHO IS THE GREAT SPIRIT?

WHO IS UNIFICATION?

WHO IS UNIQUE?

WHO IS UPLIFT?

WHO IS ULTIMATE?

WHO IS UNCONDITIONAL?

WHO IS UPGRADE?

WHO IS USEFUL?

WHO IS USER-FRIENDLY?

WHO IS UNITY?

WHO IS UNDERSTAND?

WHO IS UNDERSTANDING?

WHO IS UNDERSTOOD?

WHO IS UNIFICATION OF MIND?

WHO IS UP, WHO IS UPSKILL?

WHO IS UNBELIEVABLE?

WHO IS UNFLAPPABLE?

WHO IS UNREAL?

WHO IS UTTER AMAZEMENT?

WHO IS UNABASHED?

WHO IS UNABASHED PLEASURE?

WHO IS UNBEARABLY CUTE?

WHO IS UNHURRY?

WHO IS UNBELIEVABLE?

WHO IS UNFLAPPABLE?

WHO IS UNREAL?

WHO IS UTTER AMAZEMENT?

WHO IS UP-LEVELED?

WHO IS VITALITY?

WHO IS VALUE?

WHO IS VALUES?

WHO IS VALUABLE?

WHO IS VIRTUOUS?

WHO IS VALID?

WHO IS VERIFY?

WHO IS VERY?

WHO IS VIABLE?

WHO IS VIRTUE?

WHO IS VICTORY?

WHO IS VICTORIOUS?

WHO IS VARIETY?

WHO IS VULNERABILITY?

WHO IS VULNERABLE?

WHO IS VIBRANT?

WHO IS VOW?

WHO IS VIM?

WHO IS VIGOR?

WHO IS VENERATION?

WHO IS VOCABULEVERAGE?

WHO IS VERSATILITY?

WHO IS UBUNTU?

WHO IS WORTH?

WHO IS WORTHY?

WHO IS WORTHINESS?

WHO IS WEALTH?

WHO IS WARM?

WHO IS WARMTH?

WHO IS WELCOME?

WHO IS WILL?

WHO IS WILLING?

WHO IS WILLINGNESS?

WHO IS WISDOM?

WHO IS WISE?

WHO IS WON?

WHO IS WONDERFUL?

WHO IS WELL-BEING?

WHO IS WHOLEHEARTEDNESS?

WHO IS WOW?

WHO IS WONDER?

WHO IS WATER?

WHO IS WELL?

WHO IS WELLNESS?

WHO IS WELFARE?

WHO IS WHOLE?

WHO IS WONDER-WORKING?

WHO IS WIN?

WHO IS WINNABLE?

WHO IS WINNING?

WHO IS WALWALUN?

WHO IS WEB OF RELATEDNESS?

WHO IS WHOLEHEARTEDLY?

WHO IS WILLING TO LEARN?

WHO IS WONDROUS?

WHO IS WORLD-BUILDER?

WHO IS WORTHINESS TO TAKE UP SPACE? WHO IS WANDERLUST?

WHO IS XO?

WHO IS X-RAY VISION?

WHO IS XENODOCHIAL?

WHO IS XFACTOR?

WHO IS XENOPHILE?

WHO IS XENIAL?

WHO IS YES?

WHO IS YOUTH?

WHO IS YOUTHFUL?

WHO IS YOUNG?

WHO IS YOUNG- AT-HEART?

WHO IS YIPPEE?

WHO IS YAY?

WHO IS YEARN?

WHO IS YEA?

WHO IS YEAH?

WHO IS YUMMY?

WHO IS YEN?

WHO IS YESABILITY?

WHO IS YUGEN?

WHO IS YARAANA?

WHO IS YESABLE?

WHO IS YOU ARE LOVED?

WHO IS YOUR TRUE VALUE?

WHO IS ZEALOUS?

WHO IS ZEAL?

WHO IS ZEST?

WHO IS ZESTY?

WHO IS ZESTFUL?

WHO IS ZIPPY?

WHO IS ZING?

WHO IS ZAPPY?

WHO IS ZANY?

WHO IS ZEST FOR LIFE?

WHO IS ZAJEBISCIE?